NAUGHTY GIRL

A Sex Guide To What Men Want

ROBIN BLACK

Contents

Introduction	v
1. Sexual Tension	1
2. Playing With Yourself	5
3. The Magic Toys	7
4. Taking it Outside the Bedroom	11
5. Sex In Public	15
Introduction	21
6. Today's Dating World	23
7. Tips To Find The Right Match	33
8. Fun First Dates	35
9. The 2nd Part Of The First Date	38
10. Spontaneous Second Dates	40
11. The Third Date	42
12. Long-Term Dating	44
13. Extra Long-Term Dating	47
Afterword	51

Introduction

Sex is a normal function of EVERY human being. People love sex and were designed to have sex for pleasure, which is one of the unique qualities of humans. This book goes into detail about sex positions, dirty pleasures, and erotic, sexy situations that will get you hot and turned on.

Sex was meant to be had in the bedroom AND other places that will be disclosed in this book. It is still a "hush-hush" topic to talk about, although society is making it more common to talk about nowadays.

Sex keeps relationships alive. This book was designed to get you excited about sex and explore a wide range of new options and places for you to have sex because you love it. It includes places to have sex in public (and positions that work), as well as creative places and positions to get extra stimulated at home.

1

Sexual Tension

It doesn't matter why you want to have sex. You are wielding the power to conquer your sexual partner through the act. Nobody wants to be sloppy, especially during sex. You want to be excellent and improve in bed, just like any sexually active human being. You may want to have a porn star's talent to impress your partner or you may just want to try something new to spice it up.

Sex is exciting and mysterious. You can never predict what might happen next. Every touch and every kiss can make anyone's libido rise. Every soothing push can throw you into a spiraling sensation that can make you scream into oblivion. You throw yourself into the pleasure of having sex without thinking of anything except how good sex is and the anticipation of having an orgasm.

However, sex is not *just* about the act. Every sexual detail included in the journey to orgasm is as important as the position you and your partner use while having sex. The simple teases can build up the urge and make the orgasm more out of this world. The following are sure ways on making your partner crave for that carnal loving:

- **Sexting** – You can never tell when the urge to have sex comes, pun intended. Text your partner naughty details about what you're feeling right now. Message your partner what you're wearing and leave everything to your partner's imagination. Tell your partner what you want to do when you meet up; like how you'll tear off his/her clothes and you're going to make it the best sex ever. Include details on the surprises you planned for the night and make your partner so horny, he/she would want to eat you right now.
- **Tease** – Sometimes, it is more exhilarating to ALMOST get something. Flaunt your body in your underwear while wearing a seductive glance. Visuals are important to seduce your partner and not making him/her see your body will make him/her be eager to tearing your remaining clothes off you. The anticipation will drive your lover insane until he/she can't take it anymore.
- **Ambiance** – Set the environment into the theme you want your carnal loving to be. If you want it extreme and hard, prepare things that are associated with it like whips and handcuffs. If you want it to be romantic, set up candles or petals on the bed. You can also spritz some scents to fill the room with the mood you are attaining. Play some music appropriate to the theme of the night.
- **Porn** – Believe it or not, watching porn together can be very stimulating and may make you sexually out of control. The anticipation of doing what the actors are doing in the video

can make you go nuts! You won't be able to wait for the end of the movie to tear your partner's clothes off and mimic the actions the porn stars do. You can even follow what the stars do and go out of you and your partner's safe zone.
- **The legs** – You may or may not know how the insides of the thighs can be so sensitive. If you are out, maybe having dinner, try to caress your partner's inner thighs. You may slip your hand upward towards his/her sexual area if your hand is properly concealed. The anticipation would be too much that you may not even finish your dessert. You will be the dessert.
- **Trails** – Leave clues leading to where you plan to have sex at. Make it like a treasure hunt, with you being the treasure. Leave things like a handcuff, underwear, blindfold, or something that may remind the both of you about the first time you had sex with each other.
- **Be the boss** – Bossing around your partner regarding sex can sometimes turn the mood on. Grab your partner's hand and order him/her to touch you anywhere on your body. Do this seductively so that your partner won't think that you are being rude to him/her.
- **Reminisce** – While with your partner, share stories about how you had sex with each other. Imagine the times you had the best sex and mentally arouse each other. You may use explicit words to stimulate the both of you. You may mimic what happened during the sex both of you are visualizing about.
- **Control** – The eagerness adds up each time

you control yourself and your partner. Do not give up and tease both of you until you can't take it anymore. The sensation you would be having during sex would be like the both of you are imploding.

2

Playing With Yourself

Before you have sex you should know how to please yourself. You wouldn't enjoy having sex with someone unless you know what makes you come. Knowing what to do when your sexual partner isn't around is important to satisfy yourself in times when the urge arises.

Explore your body and determine the area of your body that is most sensitive. Play with them until you reach orgasm. You can try to position your body to help you angle your hand. You may go on fours and have fun with yourself. You may lie on your back and have your knees bent while playing with yourself. You can also try to squat if it would help you achieve that orgasm you've been craving for. Thrust your hips if you feel the need to. Find that sensitive spot and tell your partner about it on your next sexual encounter. Communication is the key for both of you to enjoy each other's bodies.

Apart from masturbating with your hands, you may use some toys to help you reach orgasm. Go to a local sex store and find a toy perfect for your needs. If you are too shy to go inside a sex store, you may search online and have it delivered. Experiment with the toy and go beyond your safe zone.

Aside from the toys, there are also other materials to help you masturbate. You can use lube if you feel like your vagina's being dry. Masturbating while your vagina is dry is dangerous since you might scratch yourself and it might lead to an infection. You may also put lube on your toy as long as it is waterproof. Aside from its ability to decrease the pain you feel from friction, some lubes have chemicals in them that may help you reach orgasm. Some may make you feel hotter down there, and some makes you cooler. Either way, orgasm is easier and medically safer when using a lube.

Pornography isn't only for men. It can also be for women. Either way, watching porn is a sure way to be stimulated and reach orgasm. It may intensify your experience while masturbating, and you can even imagine your partner as the lead in the porn.

Apart from pornographic materials, there are also sex books called erotica. This utilizes an individual's imagination and let it work its wonders. Imagination is always needed during masturbation to push you further into orgasm. However, not everyone can be stimulated by erotica novels. Find something that you think may make your horny. It may be sex tape of you and your partner, or anything that would make you hot.

3

The Magic Toys

Having sex with someone is fun! Even just the thought of having sex can make your body temperature go wild. Plain, old missionary can make you orgasm but it won't always give you the thrill you crave for when having sex. You should always spice up your sex life to make it more interesting, not dull and boring. Know different positions that will make you and your partner scream like there is no tomorrow. You may make sex hot and naughty but there is something with using sex toys that brings something new and exciting to you sex life. There is a vast number of sex toys you can use during love-making, and here are some of the best ones.

- Massager – You shouldn't go straight into sex. Foreplay is important to let the both of you crave for penetration. Teasing is always a great thing to increase the anticipation and to gradually go through the process of love-making. Familiarize yourselves about the

vibrations of the toy and slowly give in into its prowess.
- The Rabbit – This isn't just for female masturbation. It can also be used during cunnilingus to complement the sensation felt by the woman from the man's tongue. This toy is flexible since it can also be used on men. It is an effective stimulator for the nipples, shaft, scrotum, clitoris, and even both of your thighs. Familiar goosebumps, just like when you are having an orgasm, would be felt when using this toy on each other's sensitive spots.
- Cock Rings – These are used by men during sex. They vibrate, which stimulates the man's shaft, and usually has a rabbit included, which also arouses the woman. Cock rings can also be placed on the fingers. Place it on multiple fingers and let it vibrate on the woman's clit while fingering her. Dual stimulation can be achieved through touching the G-spot and the clitoris.
- Butt Plugs – Although rarely used, people who are fond of something inside their anus can be very stimulated with this toy. It can be used all throughout the intercourse or only during parts of it. Most people who like to have anal sex are more inclined to using butt plugs as an additional form of stimulation.

Some of these toys are meant to stimulate sensitive areas of the body. However, there are also sex toys that aren't meant to stimulate but to hurt. BDSM, or Bondage, Discipline, Sadism, and Masochism, is widely practiced nowadays. The thrill felt while being hurt, known as masochism, arouses some people. Being a dominant and having fun when someone is hurt, also known as sadism, is actually a turn on for some people. For this scenario to be effective during sex, one must be a sadist, and the other should be a masochist. It wouldn't work if both have the same fetish. Paraphernalia used during sex between a sadist, and masochists are as follows:

- **Blindfold** – This is the most basic object used during BDSM sex. Anticipating or giving a sexual action arouses a masochist, or sadist respectively.
- **Chains** – Being held captive is one of the sexual games played during BDSM sex.
- **Whips** – Inflicting or receiving pain is a fetish for people who enjoy BDSM. The more it hurt, the more they are aroused and enjoying.
- **Spreaders** – This makes the wearer unable to move his/her feet.
- **Golden Showers** – Some people's fetish are to be peed or to pee on someone. The sight of it arouses both individuals who are into BDSM.
- **Cock and Ball Torture** – This play involves anything painful inflicted on a man's genitals, including the eggs.
- **Electrostimulation** – Devices are used to gently electrocute an individual, usually on the genitals, to arouse him/her.
- **Pegging/Strap-ons** – The use of strap-ons has been known as a sexual activity by lesbians. However, this can also be used when a man's fetish is to have something inside his anus. A strap-on is then used by the woman to peg the man in the anus.

- **Suspension** – Having sex while suspended either with a rope or on the wall is arousing for some people. Among other BDSM plays, this is considered to be most dangerous since parts of the body are tied and it may cause nerve compression that can lead to permanent damage in an individual's body.
- **Wax Play** – Melted wax is poured onto an individual's skin as a part of foreplay.

These toys and paraphernalia can only help as long as you allow it to. You need to relax and enjoy each other's company. Remember that these are just an addition to the pleasure both of you would feel during sex.

4

Taking it Outside the Bedroom

The bedroom is where couples usually have sex. Lying on the bed is comfortable for both parties and a variety of positions can be done on and beside the bed. However, the bedroom cannot always cater to your needs, especially if you want to spice things up. This book is all about going out of your boundaries, which means that you should also have sex outside the bedroom. Here are some places in the house you may have sex, and the positions you may do in it.

- **Bathroom** – The most common room to have sex in aside from the bedroom. Having the water trickle on both of your skin adds excitement on the both of you. A lot of positions may be done in bathroom. Fellatio can be given in the bathroom with the woman kneeling and the man standing up. You can also penetrate by entering from the back with the woman's palms on the wall. The man may also carry the woman and steady himself against the wall if he can. The woman may lift her leg up to let the penis penetrate deeper.

You may also have sex inside the hot tub. Use the bubbles to your satisfaction. You may do doggy style but make sure that you have rubber mats on the tub. You might slip and hit your head if both of you won't be careful.

If having sex in either the shower or the hot tub is hard for the both of you, put the toilet cover on, let the man sit and make the woman straddle the man. It is an easier version of a cowgirl since the floor assists the woman's legs. Having sex in the bathroom is fun. The addition of steam makes it sexier inside. Just remember to be careful since the bathroom is a magnet for accidents.

- **Kitchen and Dining Room** – This room is another favorite since food can be used as paraphernalia during sex. One may lie down on the table. Whipped cream or ice cream is a favorite to be spread over the body. The cream will then be licked to turn on the other. Trails may even be made with the ending as the sex of the receiver. Similar positions can be made in the kitchen such as doggy style while standing up, and carrying the woman against the wall. You can also go the usual way of letting the woman sit on the counter and the man penetrating while standing up. It's like carrying the woman against the wall. The only difference is the woman would be sitting on the counter. Have some fun with food inside your chiller and use it to your advantage.

- **Living Room** – What better way to have sex than the couch? The narrowness of the couch would force the both of you to be nearer each other. You may spoon, go missionary, or let the man enter from the back while the woman is facing down. You may also try cowgirl and reverse cowgirl. Having a leg on the floor may help in balancing yourselves. You may also have sex standing up and let the woman use the armrest or the back of the couch to support the both of you. Let the man enter from behind and grab the woman's hips for support. The pillows can also be brought from the bedroom to the living room as an added support. If both of you are lying down, you can put it on the woman's back when doing missionary for deeper penetration.
- **Balcony** – Why not take the risk and expose yourself? Having sex at the balcony and feeling the adrenaline rush brought by the fear of getting caught adds extra excitement and pleasure to both of you. You may place a carpet or rug on the floor to make both of you comfortable. Treat the floor as your bed and have sex as if you're in a private room. Moan and shout if you like; this would help in the excitement and the fear of getting caught.
- **Laundry Room** – You never thought a washer can actually help you reach orgasm? Try laying the woman on top of the machine and let the man penetrate standing up. The vibrations produced by the washer helps stimulate the woman more. You can also use the dryer as an alternative. Instead of the

vibration, the extra warmth from the dryer can make things in the room sexier.
- **Entryway** – The excitement coming from the fear of having someone enter and seeing both of you in a compromising position can feel extremely sexy. You can use the wall as support while the man is entering from behind. If there are desks, let the woman hold on to it while doing doggy style standing up. Additional points for sexiness if there is a mirror around. Don't be ashamed to look at it and stimulate yourself as you reach your orgasm.

These aren't the only rooms in your house you could have sex in. You may have your own office or a garden. Wouldn't it be lovely to have sex amongst the flowers? Be creative and think dirty. Do not hesitate to experiment with your partner.

5

Sex In Public

It's fun to have sex inside the house. However, variety is needed if both of you already had sex on every square inch of your house. Go out and experience more thrill than your balcony. You can even go to some place crowded if you really enjoy the excitement of getting caught. Here are some of the places you can have sex outside your house:

- **Car** – Park somewhere public. You may give oral sex while the front seats are reclined. Sex can also be done at the back of a car with the back of the front seats pushed into the front. An easy way to have sex in the car is when the girl is on top while in the front seat. Cowgirl or reverse cowgirl can be done with the seat reclined.
- **Fitting Room** – Having sex in a fitting room is similar to having sex in a bathroom. The advantage of having sex in a fitting room is the full size mirror which can make you see what

both of you are doing. The additional visual aid can make both of you more aroused.
- **Movie Theater** – A lot of people know that things happen inside the movie theater. You may hear soft moaning coming from the back while the movie is rolling. It doesn't mean that you should just listen to it and do nothing. Gently move you hand towards your partner legs. Stimulate him/her and if possible, insert your hand inside his/her underwear. Play with his/her sex until both of you can't control it anymore. If the armrests could be lifted, lift it and perform fellatio. If penetration is desired, find the toilet and do the deed. Lock the door if possible, or leave it open for the extra thrill.
- **The Playground** – This place is meant for children's enjoyment. But aren't we all children inside? Use it during night time to avoid inflicting trauma to a child. The swing can be used as support for the woman and do doggy style standing up. You can let the woman place her torso onto the seat and grab hold of the chain. If you are into bondage, use the monkey bars as a suspender and have fun with it.
- **A Public Bathroom** – If both of you are up for it, a public bathroom is the way to go. Knowing that having sex inside a cubicle and creating a line of people waiting to use the toilet makes is it more exhilarating. You want to have sex fast, which makes it a lot tougher than usual. You may use the toilet as support if you are up for it, or the stall walls. Be sure to clean your hands afterwards and be ready for the

people waiting outside when both of you come out with the messy sex hair.
- **The Woods** – Camp out and enjoy nature. But before that, why don't you enjoy your partner first? The silence and peace is perfect for a romantic love-making session. If you are using a tent, various positions may be performed. Missionary, dog style, spoon, and any other traditional sex positions can be done while inside a tent, or even if you are not inside a tent. Just make sure to use a rug or blanket to lie down on. You may also use a tree as support while the man is ramming on the woman.
- **Another person's house** – Technically, it is still a house, but it's not yours. The excitement of having the owner of the house suddenly see both of you doing the deed can be exhilarating. Have sex in the bedroom, bathroom, or laundry just like how you would have sex in your house. *Although, you must but be prepared in case the owner catches the both of you and decides to kick you out.*
- **Airplane Lavatory** – Join the Mile High Club and have sex in an airplane! It is hard to be discreet especially if you are in an airplane full of people. Everyone would be observing your moves and it would be hard to enter the lavatory together. To be a part of this club, book a flight during the night. Make sure that the flight is long enough for the other passengers to snooze. If you can book a seat at the back near the lavatory, it would be more discreet.

50 Dating Ideas

Introduction

Dating, Sex, and Relationships. They all go hand in hand. Today's modern bad boy considers all three. Don't be embarrassed or ashamed about it, because it's the truth. We want dates that will eventually lead to sex and/or relationships.

Men and women think the same but we're wired so differently, meaning that we can understand each other and actually think very similar thoughts. However, the time at which we those thoughts are triggered is completely different based on the stimulus. Was it her beautiful, shiny, brown hair or was it the amazing conversation that happened during lunch?

Dating, Relationships and sex are closely connected. Traditionally, the more encounters with a particular women, the more likely sex is bound to happen, and a relationship will be formed – depending on what type of relationship the couple is seeking.

This book was designed to re-ignite things in a long-term relationship and introduce a ton of fun things to do

Introduction

for a new relationship. It talks about inexpensive to expensive dates and gives an estimated cost next to each date. Everyone relationship, whether your single or married needs to be fun, spontaneous and exciting, and this book will be your guide!

6

Today's Dating World

Every relationship starts with a simple hello, as many people say. A short greeting between two strangers can bring a sudden change to any person's life; a sign that two people begin to socialize. Dating is a way for couples to assess each other's suitability for an intimate relationship or even marriage. This is not, however, limited for younger couples as married couples can still date from time to time.

But why is dating important? Dating is a form of courtship for two people to show their love and sincerity to one another. It is composed of social activities that couples do to also maintain their companionship. If dating is not present, couples will only treat each other as colleagues instead of intimate partners. There will be no interaction and communication between the two of them even if they love one another.

WHAT IS LOVE?

Love is a pure emotion being felt by a person that do not manipulate and compromise. It is a feeling that shows kindness and care to one another. Many books may have defined love endlessly. In Neuroscience, love is involved in terms of attachment and sexual desires. Oxytocin is a chemical responsible for attachment; Dopamine, among the others, is responsible for attraction; and the sex hormones, estrogen and testosterone, are responsible for sexual desires.

Love is an instinct for human beings to grow and product offspring. It is an important factor an irrational animal lack of as love needs emotions involved. Love should always be linked with dating and couples, who are dating are expected be in love.

LOVE VS. LUST

Lust is a physical attraction that only involves in sex. It may also mean as a strong desire of the body; it can be for food, luxury and career. Lust doesn't have any emotional attachment. Therefore, it is temporary and may fade after a while. Couples who live in lust don't show any interests of living together for the rest of their lives as they only care for sexual gratification.

People may confuse love and lust at least once during their lifetime. Such infatuation has intense emotions that result to emotional rigidity. Possibilities of turning lust to love may not be positive and the chances are few. Lust can be confused with love if a person is not aware that he is only interested for self-pleasure.

Further, here are the signs of lust:

- Physical attraction – hair, skin, body build. If a person is attracted only for the body, he will not care of his partner's dreams, goals and personality.

- More sex, less talk
- Fantasy – this is more about living in a dream instead of having the same dream with a partner. People who lust enjoy a young life full of freedom, especially on the bed.
- Less meetings – people meet only for sex with another person. It would feel awkward for the two of them if they start to share secrets and philosophies that couples normally do.
- Not friends – this is more of a companionship plainly because of sex. People talk because they want to know more how to satisfy themselves physically.
- Lacks intimacy
- Obsession – some people may feel extreme neediness if their partner is not physical present. They want to know what they do and where their partner is but asking what they think and how they do never crosses their mind.
- Self-gratification – a person never cares about his partner's feelings.

STAGES OF A RELATIONSHIP or dating

There are five stages of a relationship that couples need to go through until they reach "Realistic Love."

Enchantment – Enchantment is the initial stage where couples feel ecstatic in their relationship. Anything that one of them may not like such as texting too often will be most likely ignored for a while. The couple will feel more inspired throughout their lives. They will feel more productive at work; they socialize more with their friends and family; they start to dream dreams and aim for goals and their future.

At this point, couples are filled with love and hope as they enter a new relationship. People who recently broke up with their ex may feel more contented because they think they already found the "one." Scientifically, once people feel good, the human body releases neurochemicals from the brain like Dopamine, noradrenalin and phenyl ethylamine (PEA).

Dopamine is a neurotransmitter produced in several areas of the brain like the ventral tegmental area and the substantia nigra. This hormone released by the hypothalamus is the culprit for making humans and animals excited and talkative. It can also improve cognitive alertness, working memory and mood. People can get Dopamine from foods that are rich from tyrosine like blueberries and proteins like meat, egg whites and nuts. Low Dopamine could cause depression, Attention Deficit Disorder (ADD), Restless Leg Syndrome, and Social Anxiety. Autistic people are also found to have low levels of Dopamine.

Furthermore, Noradrenaline, also known as Norepinephrine, proceeds from Dopamine by producing sweat and increased heart rate. It is released by the nerve cells from the brain as noradrenergic neurons. Noradrenergic neurons form a system called Norepinehrine system, which composes of 1500 neurons on each side of the brain. When it is activated, Norepinephrine signals the target cells in areas like the hypothalamus, spinal cord, thalamus and neocortex. Norepinehrine is responsible for a person's vigilant concentration, including recall memory, perseverance and execution. Supplement for Norepinephrine are foods that are rich in Vitamin B6 and 1-phenylalanine such as avocados, almonds, cheese, fish, lean meat and bananas. People who lack Norepinephrine may suffer from depression, hypotension, schizophrenia and Attention-deficit/Hyperactivity Disorder (ADHD).

Dopamine and Norepinephrine are released by an agent, which is Phenyl ethylamine (PEA). When more PEA is released upon initial attraction, it will make people feel more happy and in love. Phenyl ethylamine can be retrieved from sausages and cheese, contrary to the claims that chocolate contains PEA. People only feel good when eating chocolates for its sweet taste, not because it has PEA. Phenyl ethylamine belongs to the same group as amphetamines. It improves positive outlook, energy and sexual desire.

Now that the chemistry of love is understood, these three chemicals revolve in the human body by the time a person feels strong attraction to someone. The Enchantment stage is said to last for 6 to 8 months but it varies from couples to couples and may sometimes take from several weeks up to 2 to 3 years.

Power Struggle – This stage is sometimes called Disillusionment or an invitation to growth. Once the brain stopped releasing the three neurochemicals mentioned above, people will start to realize that the enchantment in their relationship is only a sort of illusion. They will start questioning their partner if he or she is the right person they want to grow old with for the rest of their lives. Couples will struggle through the challenges and may tend to neglect their relationship once they start seeing their partner's negative traits. A person may even think at one point that he is living with someone from his family that resembles his mother, sister, aunt, etc. or the ones he had trouble with. For this reason, divorce rate among couples who married at an earlier stage remains at 50 percent.

Knowledge and Awareness – Couples who are able to cope

from their conflicts during the Power Struggle Stage start to think that they already have the authority to make changes in their relationship. A person in a relationship at this stage will seek for security. Although he feels anxious and may resist in changes, he will find ways to happiness for him and his partner. He ensures their relationship to last longer by learning on how to become the right partner. Consequently, he will look for his partner's values and views for marriage. People at this stage will start learning more and more as they try to understand their partner.

Transformation – In this stage, a person will practice the skills he had learned from his partner. If conflicts arise, he will try to compromise. Couples will now start to become partners in life realizing the potential of being together. They undergo a healing process to deal with the things they endeavor from the past such as family conflicts and former lovers. Couples will be more complex to each other to create emotional safety and romance.

Real Love – This is the final stage where couples find deep respect and appreciation to one another. They find themselves as two separate individuals without losing their connection. They envision true friendship, unconditional love and partnership. Real Love is something that cannot be achieved in just four to five years. It will take more than ten years for them to embrace their wholeness. Real Love is more than a matter of responsibility, obligation and commitment. It requires willingness and perseverance to continue living together in love.

SYMPTOMS OF BEING in love

A person can fall in love as an initial reaction with someone else regardless of the race, complexion, height, weight, and personality. As they say, love has no boundaries. Here are some of the symptoms of a person who is in love:

- Thinking of a person unconsciously and subconsciously
- Lingering on the things a person use such as perfumes, shampoos and worn clothes
- Doing small, special things for the person he is attracted with even if that person is arrogant or annoying
- Showing interest about a person's life – his goals, attitude, interests and hobbies to name some
- Not minding ridiculous things and focus about the positive values of a person
- Smiling while daydreaming about him or her
- Talking about the person unstoppable
- Thinking of living with him or her under the same roof

How to cope from a previous relationship?

It may be hard for people to date someone else while they are still coping from a previous relationship that didn't work out. To others, it may take a long time for them to heal and forget the things amiss. If a person is not yet prepared to meet another special someone, it is better not to date for a while. However, people should try to love unconditionally despite the heartbreaks. A relationship may fail but it should not keep someone from loving again.

To cope from a previous relationship, a person should work on it mentally, physically and emotionally. Don't live on the past but work on the present and prepare for the future. Making oneself busy is a good head start to forget as if nothing happened. Start a new hobby, move to a new place, or join some sport clubs. Lessons from a previous relationship though should be learned and remembered. If the relationship ended from a conflict, try to review what happened and how it was dealt with; think about the things that could have done and make sure that it will never happen again.

Moving on is a part of growing up. A new relationship should be treated in a positive way and should not be used as a rebound.

WHAT IF I **just want to mingle and not commit to a serious relationship?**

Two people involved in a relationship should be aware that it's temporary. However, it is not advisable to look for any short-term relationship. Either of the two can fall in love unknown to the other person thus ends up in a one-sided love. If a person only wants to mingle, it is better for him not to think about dating first until he finds someone he is interested with.

IS ONLINE DATING FUN?

According to a research study, almost 37 percent of single people used online dating sites to look for their ideal partner. Studies also show that women are picky when looking for a person online. They also tend to look for persons who have high-paying jobs. Men, on the other hand, look for women who are young and pretty. Both genders look for similarities especially when it comes to hobbies and interests.

Online dating can be fun for some but others might feel the need of getting more physical with another.

Chances of getting married upon meeting online are relatively small compared to those who met in real life.

WHY AM I STILL SINGLE?

There are several reasons why a person is still single. Here are some:

- Pickiness – each person has his or her preferred ideal partner. He or she could be a favorite teacher, a handsome co-worker, or a famous singer. Because of a person's pickiness, potential partners are ignored.
- Defense – a previous relationship that went sour could cause trauma on a person who had a hard time dealing with it. Therefore, defensive people decide not to love ever again to avoid going through the same thing. People are taught to avoid the same mistakes. They use their defense from vulnerabilities even when it comes to love.
- Low self-esteem – people who are not confident isolate themselves from the others. They think they don't deserve to be loved so they don't pursue someone they like.
- Unnecessary attractions – a person who enters any kind of relationship just to try if it will click is something not advisable. People who do this are most likely to receive a lot of rejections because they choose people who are lesser than their ideal partners. Entering any kind of relationship is caused by having fears of solitude. A person who adjusts himself, exerting

a lot of efforts to fit in a pragmatic relationship, would only tire himself all throughout.

If a person doesn't want to be single forever, he should not force himself to fall in love just for the sake of not being alone. Loving too much or loving beyond a person could give can also be problematic because it could suffocate his partner.

7

Tips To Find The Right Match

Dating plays a major role not only on the first date but also for long-term relationships and marriage. For starters, people should not narrow down their search to find their suitable match. Through time, people should learn how to compromise and adjust to meet with the wants and needs of their partner; and of course, their partner will do the same too.

Here are some principles for finding the right match:

Avoid sexual intimacy – neither a friends-with-benefits scheme nor a one night stand will turn to a serious relationship.

Separate from parents – working independently can allow a person to think on his own. He doesn't need his parents to look over him as a whole. If this happens, he will not be able to find a suitable partner because he was depending on his parents, and may in return turn a healthy relationship into a lethal one.

Believe what other people say – a person who is attracted to someone may feel oblivious, not thinking about what others may say. For example, a boy still kept on asking a girl even though she already said he is annoying her. The boy shouldn't push too hard and believe to what she said. Every person is self-worthy, thus they should take pride that they are not at loss if they were rejected.

Aside from understanding the principles for finding the right match, keep in mind the following tips for a successful dating, such as:

- Be yourself
- Every date should be fun
- Observe good communication
- Never reveal a dating strategy
- Negotiate if needed – prove that loving is important
- Enjoy being in the relationship

There is no limit for dating. However, couples should look for the right time and mood to proceed. It's not appropriate to have a hastened date all the time or else it will wear the couple out.

8

Fun First Dates

There are many first date ideas people can come up with. Main goal is to make a conversation to get to know more each other. It's okay to combine, mix and match depending on how that someone special can enjoy and feel more comfortable. The details below are ranked from least expensive to the most expensive ones. Here are the top 15 first date ideas:

Join a volunteer rescue mission (Price range: $0)

Volunteering together at a home for the elderly can be a unique sort of a date. People who join rescue missions can also find it exciting and new. The best thing of all is it doesn't cost anything plus volunteering helped the old more happy.

Fly a Kite (Price range: $0-3)

It may sound a little bit childish but flying a kite can be fun. People can even reminisce of their childhood and share what their dreams are while doing this activity.

Roam around the local area (Price range: $0-5)

Spend some time with that special someone by taking a

long walk around the area. There may be new art shops or music store to visit or an amusement park for sightseeing. Buy hot dogs as a snack for two to boot.

Star gazing (Price range: $0-10)

A person should start familiarizing himself about the constellations in the sky to impress. Get a book from a local library or search online for possible meteor showers too. Make sure the weather is clear so there will be a lot of stars. Who knows, someone's wish might come true!

Watch a Movie (Price range: $7-9)

Contrary to popular belief, watching movies can still be a good idea for a first date. It may feel awkward not talking to each other for more than one hour and thirty minutes while watching together; it could make two people more comfortable. Not to mention enjoying a coffee to be followed after.

Play Bowling (Price range: $12-24)

Bowling is a very easy game even for starters. Two people can enjoy playing this game by creating a friendly competition plus a more relaxing conversation. What's good about bowling is that even a sophisticated woman can play this game. Bowling can be comfortable and fun.

Ice-skating (Price range: $12-30)

Ice-skating is not for figure ice-skaters only. People can share new experiences with a special someone especially for those who haven't tried skating to create a connection. It may require some practice to balance though.

Candlelight dinner at home (Price range: $14-30)

Decorate the house like a five-star hotel. Add some elegant draperies if possible that could impress a date. Cook a home-made salad and finish it off with a wine and delicious pie. Much better if there's a friend who can act as a waiter too.

Visit an Aquarium (Price range: $13-50)

Aquariums may sound childish or old-school but they are also great for a first date. New fishes and aquatic species that are colorful, toothy or amazing would keep two people talking about their interesting findings.

Visit a local zoo (Price range: $20-30)

Other people suggest that visiting a local zoo especially during winter is the best date ever. Polar bears, penguins and sea lions are good companions to spend some time along with a special someone. It is also said that they are even more active than during the warmer months.

Have a picnic (Price range: $20-40)

Best dates should be planned accordingly. It is best if the venue is held either at the garden, backyard or at a park. Prepare sandwiches, cookies and tea for a long conversation. If there is still enough time, there is an option for sightseeing.

9

The 2nd Part Of The First Date

Drink wine or coffee (Price range: $3-300)
It's never too old to ask someone for a drink or have a coffee. Wines are expensive though. Casual conversations normally start while drinking. Not to mention the venue should be a bar or a quiet coffee shop.

Eat on a new restaurant (Price range: $10-300)
Eating out can sometimes become more adventurous by going to an unusual restaurant. It could be an Asian, Indian or Vietnamese restaurant to satisfy one's palate. Who knows, it could become a favorite.

Local music gig or concert (Price range: $30-500)
Going to a gig is the best place for two music lovers to enjoy especially for a first date. Listen to the music; enjoy the drink while making a conversation. There could also be an opportunity for dancing.

Go Hiking (Price range: $0-3000)
Getting some physical activity can be a great idea for a person who wants to leave a good first impression. If there is a mountain or a hill nearby, it would be the best venue

for a first date. Hiking doesn't have to be time-consuming. It could be a brief walk to see the sunrise from the top of the hills.

Once a first date is planned, a person should know the signs if he or she is not interested. A person who is still interested to hang out with someone else would give signs such as by accepting an invitation for a second date or he or she is thanking for having a good time.

Here are the signs a woman is not interested to have a second date:

- She hasn't introduced her friends
- She would bring her friends on a date
- She doesn't answer any calls or text messages
- She talks a lot about other men
- She doesn't make any physical contact like touching or hugging

Furthermore, here are the signs a man is not interested:

- He is the main topic of the conversation
- He doesn't ask questions back like hobbies, interests, work, etc.
- He is saying offensive or mean things
- He uses his cellphone a lot
- He doesn't listen

Fear not, it's okay to give up if a first date was not successful. Don't try too hard to win that person if they don't really find something interesting. Instead, thank him or her for accepting the invitation.

10

Spontaneous Second Dates

Ghost hunting (Price range: $0)
Ghost hunting can be pretty daring for a date but it is fun and intriguing. Be ready for a flashlight and walk around a cemetery to experience the chills.

Reading books in the Library (Price range: $0)
People can share their interests by reading books. Amazing stories, famous authors and awesome characters can fascinate even a heartthrob too.

Playing Cards (Price range: $0-4)
Playing cards can be a chance to amaze a special someone. It can be played in the living room or somewhere isolated.

Going to the Beach (Price range: $0-5)
Walking near the waves at the beach is a calming way for two people to enjoy a nice conversation. It is the best venue to make a date feel more comfortable.

Go to an Arcade (Price range: $0.25-5)
Playing arcade games can be the cheapest way to impress especially when a person has a skill for PacMan. Otherwise, it's a great way to learn more how to play.

Make Ice Cream (Price range: $3-5)

Everyone can make ice cream without spending at least $20 for an ice cream maker. It can be made using the Ziploc method or the jar method. A lot of other activities can be done while waiting.

Apple Picking (Price range: $10-15)

There are some farms that allow people to pick and pay for the fruits. Normally, it would cost $0.50/lb but the admission fee is sometimes free. Best of all, people can get fresh fruits or crops during harvest season straight from the trees.

11

The Third Date

Boat Riding (Price range: $15-18)
Boat riding is good for all seasons except for winter. Riding on a romantic paddle boat is perfect for couples who want to unwind and to feel the ambiance.

Visit a Botanical Garden (Price range: $12-24)
Share childhood memories or try to identify the names of the plants to make the date more challenging.

Sing at a Karaoke Bar (Price range: $20-25)
Singing in front of the public can be a little bit tough especially for a person who is not very confident for his voice. However, he might be lucky if he finds his date is a singer.

Have a BBQ or a Cookout (Price range: $23-30)
There are people who argue about the difference of BBQ or a cookout. Either ways, as long as inviting a date is concerned and it has something to do with grilling burgers, hot dogs and meat, bring it on! This can be done even on a tight budget.

Watch a Football Event (Price range: $72-150)

Have fun and excitement by watching a football game live. Tickets are cheaper on students, however.

Buy some goods in the market (Price range: $40-200)

Going to the market together to buy groceries can be an intimate way to show interest for cooking and budget planning. Food is the best way to a man's heart, they say. And if that person can see that someone can cook for him, he may be delighted. There's no need to buy too much though, just shop for groceries that could fit enough for a week.

Go Ice Fishing (Price range: $50-$800)

A quite evening to spend ice fishing with plenty of snacks and hot cocoa can surely make a date complete. However, buying for fishing gear, a license, a hand auger and more could squeeze out more of the budget unless ice fishing has been a normal practice every winter.

12

Long-Term Dating

Once a couple enters a long-term relationship, they are also at the Power Struggle stage at the same time. Therefore, they should always find ways to spend more time with one another to improve their communication.

The danger of long-term relationships is cheating. If a person is bored with his relationship, he may start looking for another and stop dating. This is alarming and frightening for couples, which is why it is best to take an initiative to date some time.

Here are some dating ideas for long-term couples:

Watch the sunrise together (Price range: $0)

This is slightly different from hiking and it's not bad to make any repetitions since a couple has been in a relationship for a long time now. Couples may sit on top of the roof or wait on the balcony for the sunrise while drinking hot coffee.

Street fairs or festivals (Price range: $0-3)

Every city may have a fair or festival to celebrate its foundation day. It's also a great opportunity for couples to meet new friends along the way.

Do something neither of you have done before (Price range: $0-10)

Looking for something new doesn't have to be expensive. Try to recycle things from the garage and see if it can be refurbished together.

Go to Old-fashioned diners (Price range: $3-5)

Bring back old memories by going to old places or heritage including diners.

Watch a DVD at home (Price range: $3-5)

Couples find their home as a cozy place. Yet, they can still find time to enjoy without going somewhere else. Watch a DVD, or a perhaps do a movie marathon and the likes, and prepare for pop corns and sodas.

Collaborate for an evening (Price range: $13-20)

Working together is essential for couples to know their value in the relationship. Make a plan for a date at home and divide all the tasks into two. Don't forget to add TLC.

Eat an extravagant brunch together (Price range: $13-30)

Who said special meals are for the evenings only? Dress up and make a special brunch by preparing blueberry pancakes, sausages, waffles and poached eggs. A day is never complete without a heartwarming kiss.

Go to an art gallery on a weekend (Price range: $24-30)

Don't underestimate art when it comes to romance and appreciation. Sculptures and paintings may give a deeper meaning more than their looks, same with ordinary people like her who is actually extraordinary.

Go to a Shooting range (Price range: $75-150)

A shooting range is not only a place to release anger after a conflict but it could also be a challenging course for a couple. First-time visitors and beginners may take a rifle class that includes a rifle, ammunition and targets.

Go to a live concert of an unknown band (Price range: $30-500)

Create new challenges by going to an unknown music band for a change. Even if couples were able to overcome their challenges, they can still modify and rekindle activities they usually did before.

13

Extra Long-Term Dating

Married couples, like in long-term relationships, should still continue dating even after reaching "Real love." Everything is stable from this point. However, couples still need assurance that they still have a value to their partner and enjoy the rest of their lives.

Upon starting a family, couples will encounter new hindrances to continue on dating such as is having a baby, which most couples who turned to parents will be most busy. Each day, couples learn new discoveries with their baby alone instead of having them altogether. They tend to forget the importance of togetherness as a couple and they think more on caring for the baby. Eventually, they will find themselves grow apart because they don't know each other anymore. More conflicts rise and couples keep on blaming each other particularly with their career, socioeconomic status and financial problems for the sake of the baby. Further, the mother tends to ignore her husband's needs now; and since her husband will now feel lonely, he will look for alternatives aside from cheating like drinking and smoking. This could be a problematic situation for couples once a new person in their life is involved.

The second hindrance for dating among married couples is their financial status. They prioritize bills like food, rent, and other utility bills. They don't think of having an emotional attachment now or spend money for dating. Even those who have sufficient funds think more on how to expand their money instead of thinking of how to improve together as a couple.

Now some of the hindrances are identified, here are some dating ideas for married couples:

Playground date (Price range: $0)

Couples can still have a good time just like when they were young. They can play on the monkey bars, swing or slides. Watch out for accidents and a weak back though.

Tree-climbing (Price range: $0)

Tree-climbing is another activity that couples can also do for free. The best part of it is it also improves their muscles and dexterity.

Have a Sunday Crossword date (Price range: $0.30-5)

Older married couples enjoy answering crosswords on a Sunday morning more than younger adults while having a hot coffee and tasty waffles.

Watch a Drive-in movie (Price range: $5-7)

Drive-in movie theaters are cheaper than regular theaters. If a couple is already sick of watching movies at home, doing this could be a memorable experience.

Photo booth hunt (Price range: $5-10)

Some arcades have photo booths that are available for all ages. Give it a try, wear a funky wig and have fun making faces.

Eat a lot of sweets (Price range: $8-20)

Ever wonder what happens once a person eats a lot of

candies? Try to satisfy a sweet tooth. Be careful of the sugar level.

Opera or a musical show (Price range: $25-35)

Looking for a sophisticated date? Try for an opera or a music show. It is livelier than a movie theater.

Decorate a Christmas tree together (Price range: $20-80)

It's nice to know that married couples are now able to decorate their Christmas tree together. Buy for a real tree because they are cheaper than the fake ones.

Random restaurant date (Price range: $30-100)

Take a pick from all nearby restaurants and act as if a food critique upon eating the food they serve. It's like a trial-and-error for married couples who also like to date as if it's for the first time.

Hot air ballooning (Price range: $1050-1100)

Once a married couple is able to save more, they can come up of having a private moment in the air. Hot air balloons are very expensive but its experience may last for a lifetime.

Afterword

Dating doesn't have to be pricey just for two people to be together. There are many ways to express love and affection aside from dating.

Couples should avoid complacency and apathy in their relationship because it could kill even the good memories. They should act more than intimate partners.

The next step is to take action for a relationship to survive. Don't waste even for a minute!

Even married couples experience new activities.

Thanks for reading!

www.ingramcontent.com/pod-product-compliance
Lightning Source LLC
Chambersburg PA
CBHW070035040426
42333CB00040B/1686